ACROSS THE WIDE DARK SEA

The Mayflower Journey

Jean Van Leeuwen *pictures by* Thomas B. Allen

Dial Books for Young Readers 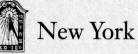 New York

For John E. Charlton, Samuel Gavril, and Eva Kaner Gavril—
Travelers all to a new world   J.V. L.

To new beginnings and happy endings, yours, mine,
and especially for Victoria Patricia   T. B. A.

The author would like to acknowledge the assistance of Plimoth Plantation in
doing research for this book, and thank Carolyn Freeman Travers,
Director of Research, for checking the manuscript for accuracy.

Published by Dial Books for Young Readers
A Division of Penguin Books USA Inc.
375 Hudson Street
New York, New York 10014

Design by Nancy R. Leo
Printed in Hong Kong
First Edition
3 5 7 9 10 8 6 4 2

Library of Congress Cataloging in Publication Data
Van Leeuwen, Jean.
Across the wide dark sea / by Jean Van Leeuwen; pictures by Thomas B. Allen.
p.   cm.
Summary: A boy and his family endure a difficult nine-week journey across
the ocean and survive the first winter at Plymouth Plantation in Massachusetts.
ISBN 0-8037-1166-2.—ISBN 0-8037-1167-0 (lib. bdg.)
1. Pilgrims (New Plymouth Colony)—Juvenile fiction.
[1. Pilgrims (New Plymouth Colony)—Fiction.
2. Massachusetts—History—New Plymouth, 1620–1691—Fiction.]
I. Allen, Thomas B. (Thomas Burt), 1928– ill. II. Title.
PZ7.V3273Ac 1995 [E]—dc20 91-16926 CIP AC

The full-color artwork was prepared with charcoal, pastel, and colored pencils.
It was then scanner-separated and reproduced in red, blue, yellow, and black halftones.

I STOOD CLOSE TO MY FATHER as the anchor was pulled
dripping from the sea. Above us, white sails rose against a bright
blue sky. They fluttered, then filled with wind. Our ship began to move.

My father was waving to friends on shore. I looked back at their
faces growing smaller and smaller, and ahead at the wide dark sea.
And I clung to my father's hand.

We were off on a journey to an unknown land.

The ship was packed tight with people—near a hundred, my father said. We were crowded below deck in a space so low that my father could barely stand upright, and so cramped that we could scarcely stretch out to sleep.

Packed in tight, too, was everything we would need in the new land: tools for building and planting, goods for trading, guns for hunting. Food, furniture, clothing, books. A few crates of chickens, two dogs, and a striped orange cat.

Our family was luckier than most. We had a corner out of the damp and cold. Some had to sleep in the ship's small work boat.

The first days were fair, with a stiff wind.

My mother and brother were seasick down below. But I stood on deck and watched the sailors hauling on ropes, climbing in the rigging, and perched at the very top of the mast, looking out to sea.

What a fine life it must be, I thought, to be a sailor.

One day clouds piled up in the sky. Birds with black wings circled the ship, and the choppy sea seemed angry.

"Storm's coming," I heard a sailor say.

We were all sent below as the sailors raced to furl the sails.

Then the storm broke. Wind howled and waves crashed. The ship shuddered as it rose and fell in seas as high as mountains. Some people were crying, others praying. I huddled next to my father, afraid in the dark.

How could a ship so small and helpless ever cross the vast ocean?

The sun came out. We walked on deck and dried our clothes. But just when my shoes felt dry at last, more clouds gathered.

"Storm's coming," I told my father.

So the days passed, each one like the last. There was nothing to do but eat our meals of salt pork, beans, and bread, tidy up our cramped space, sleep when we could, and try to keep dry. When it was not too stormy, we climbed on deck to stretch our legs. But even then we had to keep out of the sailors' way.

How I longed to run and jump and climb!

Once during a storm a man was swept overboard. Reaching out with desperate hands, he caught hold of a rope and clung to it.

Down he went under the raging foaming water.

Then, miraculously, up he came.

Sailors rushed to the side of the ship. Hauling on the rope, they brought him in close and with a boat hook plucked him out of the sea. And his life was saved.

Storm followed storm. The pounding of wind and waves caused one of the main beams to crack, and our ship began to leak.

Worried, the men gathered in the captain's cabin to talk of what to do. Could our ship survive another storm? Or must we turn back?

They talked for two days, but could not agree.

Then someone thought of the iron jack for raising houses that they were taking to the new land. Using it to lift the cracked beam, the sailors set a new post underneath, tight and firm, and patched all the leaks.

And our ship sailed on.

For six weeks we had traveled, and still there was no land in sight. Now we were always cold and wet. Water seeping in from above put out my mother's cooking fire, and there was nothing to eat but hard dry biscuits and cheese. My brother was sick, and many others too.

And some began to ask why we had left our safe homes to go on this endless journey to an unknown land.

Why? I also asked the question of my father that night.

"We are searching for a place to live where we can worship God in our own way," he said quietly. "It is this freedom we seek in a new land. And I have faith that we will find it."

Looking at my father, so calm and sure, suddenly I too had faith that we would find it.

Still the wide dark sea went on and on. Eight weeks. Nine.

Then one day a sailor, sniffing the air, said, "Land's ahead." We dared not believe him. But soon bits of seaweed floated by. Then a tree branch. And a feather from a land bird.

Two days later at dawn I heard the lookout shout, "Land ho!"

Everyone who was well enough to stand crowded on deck. And there through the gray mist we saw it: a low dark outline between sea and sky. Land!

Tears streamed down my mother's face, yet she was smiling. Then everyone fell to their knees while my father said a prayer of thanksgiving.

Our long journey was over.

The ship dropped anchor in a quiet bay, circled by land. Pale yellow sand and dark hunched trees were all we saw. And all we heard was silence.

What lurked among those trees? Wild beasts? Wild men? Would there be food and water, a place to take shelter?

What waited for us in this new land?

A small party of men in a small boat set off to find out. All day I watched on deck for their return.

When at last they rowed into sight, they brought armfuls of firewood and tales of what they had seen: forests of fine trees, rolling hills of sand, swamps and ponds and rich black earth. But no houses or wild beasts or wild men.

So all of us went ashore.

My mother washed the clothes we had worn for weeks beside a shallow pond, while my brother and I raced up and down the beach.

We watched whales spouting in the sparkling blue bay and helped search for firewood. And we found clams and mussels, the first fresh food we had tasted in two months. I ate so many I was sick.

Day after day the small party set out from the ship, looking for just the right place to build our settlement.

The days grew cold. Snowflakes danced in the wind. The cold and damp made many sick again. Drawing his coat tightly around him, my father looked worried.

"We must find a place," he said, "before winter comes."

One afternoon the weary men returned with good news. They had found the right spot at last.

When my father saw it, he smiled. It was high on a hill, with a safe harbor and fields cleared for planting and brooks running with sweet water. We named it after the town from which we had sailed, across the sea.

It was December now, icy cold and stormy. The men went ashore
to build houses, while the rest of us stayed on board ship. Every fine
day they worked. But as the houses of our settlement began to rise,
more and more of our people fell sick. And some of them died.

It was a long and terrible winter.

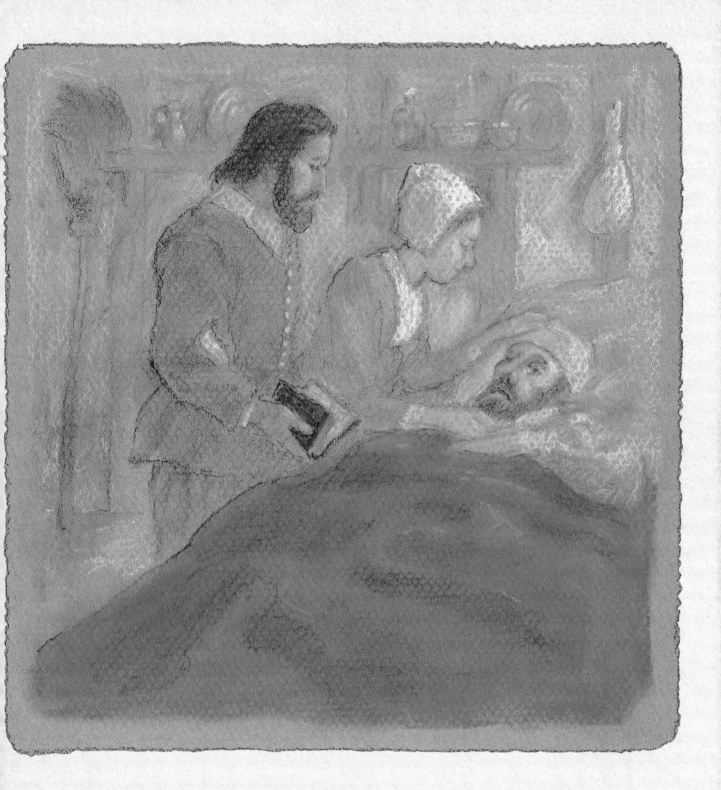

We had houses now, small and rough. Yet the storms and sickness went on. And outside the settlement, Indians lurked, seldom seen but watching us.

My father and mother nursed the sick, and my father led prayers for them. But more and more died. Of all the people who had sailed for the new land, only half were left.

One morning in March, as I was gathering firewood, I heard a strange sweet sound. Looking up, I saw birds singing in a white birch tree.

Could it be that spring had come at last?

All that day the sun shone warm, melting the snow. The sick rose from their beds. And once more the sound of axes and the smell of new-split wood filled the air.

"We have done it," my father said. "We have survived the winter."

But now the Indians came closer. We found their arrows, and traces of their old houses. We caught sight of them among the trees. Our men met to talk of this new danger. How could so small a settlement defend itself?

Cannons were mounted on top of the hill, and the men took turns standing guard. Then one day an Indian walked into the settlement. Speaking to us in our own language, he said, "Welcome."

Our Indian friend came back and brought his chief. We all agreed to live in peace.

And one of the Indians stayed with us, teaching us where to find fish in the bubbling brooks, and how to catch them in traps, and how to plant Indian corn so that next winter we would have enough to eat.

My father and I worked side by side, clearing the fields, planting barley and peas and hills of corn.

Afterward I dug a garden next to our house. In it we planted the seeds we had brought from home: carrots and cabbages and onions and my mother's favorite herbs, parsley, sage, chamomile, and mint.

Each day I watched, until something green pushed up from the dark earth. My mother laughed when she saw it.

"Perhaps we may yet make a home in this new land," she said.

On a morning early in April our ship sailed back across the sea. We gathered on shore to watch it go. The great white sails filled with wind, then slowly the ship turned and headed out into the wide dark sea.

I watched it growing smaller and smaller, and suddenly there were tears in my eyes. We were all alone now.

Then I felt a hand on my shoulder.

"Look," my father said, pointing up the hill.

Spread out above us in the soft spring sunshine was our settlement: the fields sprouting with green, the thatch-roofed houses and neatly fenced gardens, the streets laid out almost like a town.

"Come," my father said. "We have work to do."
With his hand on my shoulder we walked back up the hill.

Author's Note 🌿

THIS IS THE STORY OF ONE VOYAGE, BUT ALSO OF MANY.
Some took place hundreds of years ago, others in a time our grandparents can remember. Some are taking place even today. In all of them, families left behind everything they knew and bravely set out to make a new life in a new land. It is because of this that I have used no names in my story.

But the voyage I have described was a special one in American history. For the time was 1620, and the ship was the Mayflower. The place where it first landed was Cape Cod, on the eastern tip of Massachusetts. And the settlement was named Plymouth Plantation after the town of Plymouth, England, from which the ship sailed. This was one of the first permanent European settlements in the unexplored wilderness of North America.

This is a true story. We know because one of the ship's passengers wrote about the voyage and the early years of Plymouth Plantation. His name was William Bradford, and he became governor of the colony. Because of him we know how many people sailed on the Mayflower, and most of their names. We know how the new land looked to them, how they explored it and chose the place to build their settlement. We know about their terrible winter of sickness and their spring of hope, when two friendly Indians, Samoset and Squanto, taught them the skills they would need to survive. Both Indians spoke English. Samoset had learned a few words from English fishermen, while Squanto, who became the settlers' special friend, had been kidnapped by an English ship's captain and lived in England for a time.

Approximately thirty of the Mayflower's passengers were children. I chose one of them to write about. His name was Love Brewster. He was about nine years old when he sailed on the Mayflower with his parents and younger brother, whose name was Wrestling. His father, William Brewster, was one of the leaders of a religious group called "separatists," who left England to find a place where they could worship God in their own way. He became the religious leader of the colony. Love Brewster grew up in Plymouth Plantation, married, and had four children of his own.

All of this we know is true. What we do not know is how it felt to be a small boy on a small ship sailing across a vast ocean to an unknown land. In this book I have tried to see the voyage of the Mayflower as Love Brewster might have seen it. My story is imaginary, but I hope it is also true.